Sixty Years

poems by

Karen Haskell

Finishing Line Press
Georgetown, Kentucky

Sixty Years

Copyright © 2016 by Karen Haskell
ISBN 978-1-944251-73-4 First Edition
All rights reserved under International and Pan-American Copyright Conventions. No part of this book may be reproduced in any manner whatsoever without written permission from the publisher, except in the case of brief quotations embodied in critical articles and reviews.

Editor: Christen Kincaid

Cover Art: Karen Haskell

Author Photo: Karissa Mlyniec

Cover Design: Karen Haskell

Printed in the USA on acid-free paper.
Order online: www.finishinglinepress.com
        also available on amazon.com

                Author inquiries and mail orders:
                     Finishing Line Press
                       P. O. Box 1626
                 Georgetown, Kentucky 40324
                         U. S. A.

Table of Contents

Drizzle 1

Newly Wed 2

Small Battles 3

Bedtime 4

The Negative 5

Stretch Marks 6

Recruitment Office 7

The Bible: 1942 8

The Move 9

The Affair 10

Nightmare 11

Leave, 1944 12

Missing 13

Survivors 14

Perogies 15

Back 16

Next of Kin 17

Marked 18

Sixty Years 19

For Brian, Lainey, & Claudia

Drizzle

She expected rain
for a week.
Sky, mood overcast.

She slept
on the floor.
An old remedy,
an old wives' tale.

Headaches, backaches
stomach aches
cured.

Still she could feel
a baby.
Heartbeat after heartbeat
after heartbeat.

A week gone by
splintered, sore
she slept.
Rainwater settled in pots.

Drip-drop.
Thump-thump.

Newly Wed

He loved her,
married her.
Uncomplicated
he worked, played ball, cards,
joked with the guys.
He meant
to bring her flowers, trinkets.
He'd come home late
to a clean house, warm bed,
and he believed
a happy wife.

Small Battles

Waged in piles of laundry,
dirty dishes,
a headache every night.
She wants to win.

Their yelling matches
end with his word.
Their bank account
expands, shrinks
with his signature.
Their trajectory fixed
like the north star.

Later she'll say: too tight,
the tiny one bedroom
on the same side of town
she always lived on.
Too tight, too close,
perhaps
too far away.

Bedtime

She sleeps crooked
legs bent under,
hands clutching pillow, blankets.
He smiles at her.

He wants to wake her,
to press his cold hands
against her expanding belly.
To put his ear there as well.

He wants to wake her
to her old self
of shy smiles
and easy handholding,
to moments of non-negotiated peace.

Instead in the corner,
he settles.
Rocks back, forth
runners scratching the floor,
wishing for a dreamless sleep.

The Negative

Again she says
like there can be an again.
From the living room, he stares.
He wants her to be something else.
Someone with a vocabulary
of "again" and "yes"
and a shrug of her shoulders.

He wants her to leave,
wants only her shadow
draped on the hardwood floor.
A picture taken out of focus.
A negative he can burn,
flinging the ashes away
in a proper burial.

Again she says.
Again, again, again.
He's still staring at her.
Hearing her.
Listening to her.
Not again.
It registers
like the click of a key in a lock.

Stretch Marks

Vinelike patterns
spread across her stomach
as if she were an old brick building
suited to ivy crawling, spiraling upward.

In the tub, she traces the lines
with her water-wrinkled finger
as if they are a language
she is just beginning to learn.

Behind her eyes she sees paintings
with huge brushstrokes in skin tones and flesh.
She wants an eraser, or white paint
to bleach everything clean.
She wants a rebirth.

Recruitment Office

The line was short.
Eight, no nine other men.
Young men
with newly grown beards,
uncalloused hands,
and sweethearts full
of optimism, heady
with God and hero worship,
ready to save
a world.

The taste
of coffee, black,
strong in his throat.
In his pocket
his wedding ring
unbroken circle of life
lies fallow, fractured
as if hollowed from
the inside out.

After heavy rain
the seeds
white and bloated
dot the soil
the growing gone.

The Bible: 1942

His is underlined
pages bent at the corner,
passages fingered, smudged.

He has seen others not make it,
exploding into single syllables
as bombs burst without notice.

His has survived rain, rivers, storms.
Each time the wet ink drying
into new images of heaven and hell.

He thinks about mailing it,
this proof of faith, to her.

About sending it unmarked
in brown paper,
stamped with the army seal.

He thinks about her,
eight months pregnant
at Sunday mass
in the heat of summer
brown hair braided
to the nape of her neck,
a wide brim hat
and soft silk stockings.

The Move

I.

Like other mothers,
she'd place her hand there
walking out of church,
down the street to the corner store.
A flutter, then a kick
hard, pushing.
Unconsciously her small hand
would slide down, around
checking.

II.

She screamed.
The baby didn't.

The silence still.

III.

The bus moved slowly
past farmlands, plains
in between mountains.

She hugged
her one suitcase
tight on her lap.

The Affair

Guilt lived with her
like a lover
except it never caressed her
or whispered sweet nothings.
It was abusive, shattering,
left new scars daily.

She never kicked it out,
never left herself.
They were a package deal.

It followed her
like a shadow,
obvious in daylight,
deadly in the dark.

When they spoke,
she wept.
She had no excuses.

Nightmare

He wakes to body parts
and a baby.

Fingers, toes, legs.
The baby wordless,
whole.

It isn't new.

In foxholes,
at bars,
in the shower.

Even with eyes open
it flashes
lightning-like
repeating itself
over and over.

Leave, 1944

Instead of a marriage,
he killed men now.
The tally high,
routine, breathtaking.

It was that moment
the boundary between
being here
and not here
that was familiar to him.

He was 12
the first time
he drowned.
Water sliding,
slipping in
and then out
when his father dragged
him to shore.

At 17 he tried again.
The lake still
solid with promise.
His feet, knees wet
when the boat
glided into view.

He was better at 21
when she arrived.
At the altar her veil
shielded her pink cheeks.
Her dress stretched down
the aisle. Her hand reaching
for his.

Missing

He stayed in a small, spare bedroom in his sister's two-family home. A wide porch sat on the square front lawn and in the driveway a large pink Cadillac with rosary beads looped around the rearview mirror. On neighboring porches, old men sat with cards in one hand and beer in the other, laughing with each obscene joke. On the street, dodge balls and marbles ran loose while kids hurried after the ice cream truck. He stood as straight as he could on the second of three steps, his body turned halfway between the street and the house. It was as if he had been caught mid-step by a voice he knew. And when he stood like that he could almost hear the voice, the voice of his child calling *daddy*.

Survivors

He kept them in an old cigar box
beneath a white handkerchief.
Never telling his sister
or mother that he had them.
Never taking them out,
or mentioning them,
not even when he got together with old friends.

He packed them away
in the trunk in the attic
next to his pocket bible.
It was only when the fourth
came in the mail
that he opened the trunk,
pulled out the box
and really looked at the three medals
lying side by side like dead bodies.

Perogies

On the sill, a plate. Closer it was pie, not perogies. Blueberry. He used to cook for her, for their seedling of a child. Cabbage, potato, blueberry, blackberry. Savory, sweet. Encased in a pocket of dough. She loved him best then. In that swell of a moment as he sealed each one.

Back

She's come home
to orange leaves
and a blood moon.

To that certain
uncertainty
of him, of them.

The unsaid
waxing, waning
in her throat,
on her tongue,
in her eyes.

At sunset she thinks
of summer.
The lake lighted by fireflies
yellow and dark green,
amber camp-fire dances
courting with cold light
as their soft spotlight
fades into the dawn.

She's awake long before
that brilliant snap
of sunlight hits
the morning dew.

Next of Kin

She dreams of the telegram
in army green
extended across the doorstep
like a friendly handshake.

She greets the messenger
with the knowledge
his eyes give away:
He's dead, she says.
He's dead.
Not him, but the baby.

She dreams of her son
full-grown, fighting
in another war
not the one
his parents began.

She sees him blue
eyes closed, a heart
that never beat.

Marked

He thought his own
would be unmarked
somewhere in the south of France.

This one was shaded.
The branch of a solid maple tree
jutted out just enough
to cast a shadow
across his son's name.

He stood there
half in sunlight
half in shade
until a small, familiar hand
slipped into his.

There between the two
cupped hands
where skin brushed
together and fingerprints
swirled into one,
there in that space
of touching and not touching
was a life
time.

Epilogue:
Sixty Years

Every day he brings her flowers
and two oatmeal cookies.
They converse in short silly sentences
while he pats her arm
and she twists the tablecloth
between her long fingers.

At times he moves closer to her
squinting out his spotted, scratched
glasses, looking, searching.
But the glasses are old,
the prescription no good,
his eyesight almost gone anyway.

But she recognizes his wrinkly face
and gently teasing voice.
It's his name and how
she knows him that's been forgotten.
But he's here for her.
She knows that as sure as,
as sure as what?
She really can't remember.

So instead she hums a tune
no one recognizes
and he adds what he
can to the melody.
His deep voice throwing
the whole song off key.

At exactly 4:30 he kisses her check
pressing thin lips against countless wrinkles.
The cookies are gone and
the flower petals scattered on the floor.
He can't see them and
she doesn't remember they're there.

Acknowledgments

This series began with the last poem, written while I was still an undergraduate at Wheaton College. At Wheaton my writing skills and love of literature were developed and honed by many wonderful professors, but most prominently Sue Standing and Bev Clark.

I started writing the rest of this short story in verse not long after my grandfather died in 2001. The story and characters are wholly my own but the seeds were planted by him and his experience (which he rarely talked about) as a WWII veteran.

Many of the poems in this series were conceived and nurtured during my first semester in graduate school at Sarah Lawrence College. I am thankful for the wonderful professors and writing community there.

In later years this story has been cultivated and immensely influenced by the members of Rhode Island's *Poetry Loft*. A heartfelt thanks to Bea for welcoming me into the Loft and making me a member of a fantastic tribe of writers including Jim, Nancy, Mike, Mo, Joan, Ira, Andy, Mary, Judy, & Sandra.

I have also found a home with a fantastic group of mom-writers—the 2014 cast of Listen to Your Mother – who have been wonderfully supportive.

Additionally I want to extend my sincerest thanks to Frequency Writers, in particular Darcie Dennigan. Frequency Writers bills itself as "a moving creation of the people in it." And the people that make up Frequency, both instructors and students, are generous, open-minded and passionate about the written word.

I am also extremely grateful for my incredible family who has believed in me since I started writing poems at age ten. The list includes: Susan & Mike Mlyniec, Laura Mlyniec, Matthew Mlyniec, Frank & Rose Mlyniec, Frank Mlyniec Jr, Cindy Mauch, Don & Marge White, Dawn & Lloyd Niles, Cathy Whitehead, Tom & Ann White, Gary & Nancy White, Marcia & Dan Panciera, and all my many cousins.

Thank you to my friends who I hooked into reading drafts even though they claim not to be readers of poetry (but really they are truly excellent readers): Nadia, Katie, & Emily.

Lastly thank you to my husband Brian for his support, encouragement, and willingness to jump in and help with whatever I need help with.

Karen Haskell is a graduate of Wheaton College in Norton, Massachusetts and received her MFA in writing from Sarah Lawrence College. Most recently her work appeared in print as part of *Hope Street: Nine New England Poets on Love and Loss* published by Main Street Rag, in exhibit at the Wickford Art Association's 2015 Poetry & Art Exhibit, and on stage as a member of the 2014 Listen to Your Mother Providence, RI cast. Additionally she is the 2nd place winner of the 2015 Galway Kinnell Poetry Contest. Currently she spends the majority of her time as a stay at home mom to her two daughters; she also teaches part-time in the writing department at the University of Rhode Island.

www.ingramcontent.com/pod-product-compliance
Lightning Source LLC
Chambersburg PA
CBHW060227050426
42446CB00013B/3209